The Album

PEG BOYERS

DOS MADRES
2021

DOS MADRES PRESS INC.
P.O. Box 294, Loveland, Ohio 45140
www.dosmadres.com   editor@dosmadres.com

Dos Madres is dedicated to the belief that the small press is essential to the vitality of contemporary literature as a carrier of the new voice, as well as the older, sometimes forgotten voices of the past. And in an ever more virtual world, to the creation of fine books pleasing to the eye and hand.

Dos Madres is named in honor of Vera Murphy and Libbie Hughes, the "Dos Madres" whose contributions have made this press possible.

Dos Madres Press, Inc. is an Ohio Not For Profit Corporation and a 501 (c) (3) qualified public charity. Contributions are tax deductible.

Executive Editor: Robert J. Murphy

Illustration & Book Design: Elizabeth H. Murphy
www.illusionstudios.net

Typeset in Adobe Garamond Pro, Palatino Linotype
& Apple Chancery

ISBN 978-1-953252-28-9
Library of Congress Control Number: 2021941483

First Edition
Copyright 2021 Peg Boyers
All rights reserved. No part of this book may be reproduced or transmitted in any form or by any means graphic, electronic or mechanical, including photocopying, recording, taping or by any information storage or retrieval system, without the permission in writing from the publisher.
Published by Dos Madres Press, Inc.

for Robert and our children

and for Frank

"I wish there were two more commandments.
The eleventh would be don't change.
The twelfth would be change." (Yehuda Amichai)

and for Edwin, yogi extraordinaire — with gratitude for your patience + generally exceptional humanity —

Peg Boyers
11/26/2021

TABLE OF CONTENTS

Preface vii
La Tempesta 2
The Album 4
Four Ages 8
Cubism 11
The Model Speaks 13
The Convalescent Woman in a Time of Plague . . 15
Klee in Tunisia 17
Against the Light 21
Pietà 23
Deposition 25
Frau Dürer on *Melencolia I* 27
Double Portrait 31
Margherita Sarfatti 33
I Dreamt I Was Tiger 35
Self-Portrait with a Thriftstore Cap 38
Morning Meditation 40

GARLAND OF CURING RAGAS
1. Safina 43
2. Falling Peacock in the Rain at Night 45
3. Before the Rain at Nat Mahar 49
4. Deccan Picnic with Krishna 52

The Last Wait 54
The Fate of Pleasure 57

Notes 60
Credits 61
Acknowledgements 63
About the Author 65

PREFACE

I came to writing poems relatively late in life. (My first book was published just as I was about to turn 50.) But I have been looking at paintings and sculptures—in museums, in churches, in galleries, often the same ones over and over again—ever since I moved with my family to Venice when I was twelve and later went to high school in Rome. The works of art I've studied over the decades, in many different countries, are as much a part of me as any other aspect of my past, and naturally they have found their way into my poems. They carry for me the weight of lived experience and have been a way for me to reflect on and make sense of that experience in poems.

I have wrestled with, and resisted, and finally embraced the idea of publishing my ekphrastic poems with their corresponding images. A few poet friends have assured me that the poems need no visual accompaniment, and at two public readings I have read a handful of the poems without projecting the images and felt that my audience was with me, comfortably and completely. And yet on several other occasions I have read the poems with the images projected and found that my audience was grateful to look at the images that had inspired me. Many of my own students who were present at my recent public readings have told me how important it was for them to see the works as I was reading to them.

Occasionally poets will say that they were moved to write an ekphrastic poem by the prospect of bringing a visual image to life or giving it a voice. That has never been an important motive for me. The works that accompany my poems seem to me to have more than sufficient life and to speak with a voice powerful enough to be heard by those who submit to them. In fact, my motives in writing ekphrastic poems are in no way reducible to a single impulse. The images that have moved me to write are so different from one another as to generate wildly different kinds of poems. Some of them speak in the imagined voice of the painter, others in the invented voice of a figure depicted in the painting, still others in a voice somewhat like my own. In all of them I have sought to evoke a surface while excavating and elaborating a narrative, however fragmentary.

Each of the poems in this book, then, relates to a painting or sculpture, but is by no means an "illustration." In writing the poems I have allowed myself to move well beyond the visible parameters of the images, exploring what seem to me leads and implications, traveling out as far as seemed plausible and compelling while at the same time never quite abandoning the constraint embodied in each image. The poems are unified only in the sense that each relates to what seems to me a worthy "original." Taken together the poems offer something of a representative, if miscellaneous, account of the interests, passions and fears of their author. Nothing more, nothing less.

The Album

La Tempesta*

For years we told ourselves we might avoid it,
as if it hadn't been there all along, buried
beneath the ruins we thought quaint, picturesque.

2

Even the lightning crashing menace across the sky
we refused to take seriously.

Instead, we bought the souvenir tie in the museum shop
and laughed at how, out of context, the electric
streak adorning it was

just a smear of yellow across an expanse of lagoon-green silk,
the rest of the story brewing
off-stage, out of view.

Like Giorgione, we trained our focus on the lush foreground
(woman nursing infant by stream; handsome voyeur eyeing her)
preferring to ignore the rest:

the deaths accumulating among the old and the unlucky young,
illnesses and overdoses claiming them relentlessly
with each passing season.

But the ruins in the distance—the dilapidated bridge to the
approaching night—beckon with a steady, patient
insistence

toward the lightning, the inexorably tormented sky.

So we gather our cloaks —
not against the storm (which *will* arrive)
but against our dread of the storm.

*after *La Tempesta* by Giorgione, 1504

The Album*

He can still smell their powder, the morning
cologne aging in the dove gray afternoon.
Under their heavy dresses, the familiar musk—
sweat and body odor beginning to surface.

And where was he, why does
he not see himself in the scene?

It must have been summer, the white hydrangea
and wine-dark roses crowding their invisible vases,
blood reds and garnet fading
with the hours into shriveled cerise
and dull currant. They long for the fields.
He too longs for the fields.
In the stifling living room where
yesterday's poppies droop
their melancholy into the shade he, too, droops
and the shade affords no solace.

The women are busy ignoring the season, the heat—
and him. Do they even notice
his presence, his isolation,
his separate superfluity?

In this house of women, the lone male
is lonesome.
Even the maid in her black apron turns
away, fiddles with a bouquet on an upper shelf,
while the sisters converge around Mamá.
She is telling and retelling the ancient stories, passing
on the lore. They lean into her, absorbing
her memories, making them their own
as they pass the album from lap to lap.

The album is a hand-made thing:
buff poster board pages stuffed between
two plywood sheets sewn
with a thick leather strap. Pasted
on the cover is a globe, ringed with five
headshots of smiling babes.

His own fair head bobs over outer Mongolia.
He is the last born, the baby, the boy outsider,
in a clan of brunettes, the only blond.

Flecks of flint-dusk and pearl dot the scene.
Furniture/flowers/figures dissolve
into one another, the patterns blending, faces
and fabric becoming one. In their casual elegance
like the wall paper they resemble

the old complications resolve, complement
each other in the swirl
he cannot enter.

He is dreaming the impossible
dream, the old compulsion to unite
what is disparate, blend
with the surround. He would smudge
the lines of separation if he could,
obliterate difference.

If he looks back, past the years
to his childhood, he can see
his own boy face, not yet apart, but
slipping away. How did it happen?

He studies the photographs for clues, for signs
of his future redundancy. If he looks
hard, he can see it coming, negative space
already stalking the picture plane.

*after *The Album* (1895) by Edouard Vuillard

Four Ages *

Today, I'm the one with no clothes. The Baby. The Accident.
The bitter exhibitionist, the Adolescent, arrested
on canvas. My sister to the left—how long

before I, like her, become the perfect embodiment
of Youthful Womanhood, complacent
in my satins and silks. *Go ahead, strip*,

she dares me. So I do—to prove my valor and win
that orange ribbon she's pledged me for my hair.
I'd like to strangle her with it.

Worse, to my right, Maturity
and Middle Age await, draped
in marmish prints and spinster's black.

Our painter father's put us here, littering
the ground with sundry profundities.
Symbol and allegory: I hate them all.

That distinctive pheasant over there
has his Meaning, too, no doubt.
Listen: his wrinkled gullet's clucking

something sweet. And intentional.
I like his glassy eyes—his flirty feathers.
Could it be that he is really Jove

and I'm to be his Leda? Is he more
or less than
the myth he represents?

If I invite him for a dip
will he swim? How will he paddle
with those web-less chicken feet?

I had hoped for a swan,
with a long hard neck
and a wingspan I could love.

*after *Le Signorine* (1912) by Felice Casorati

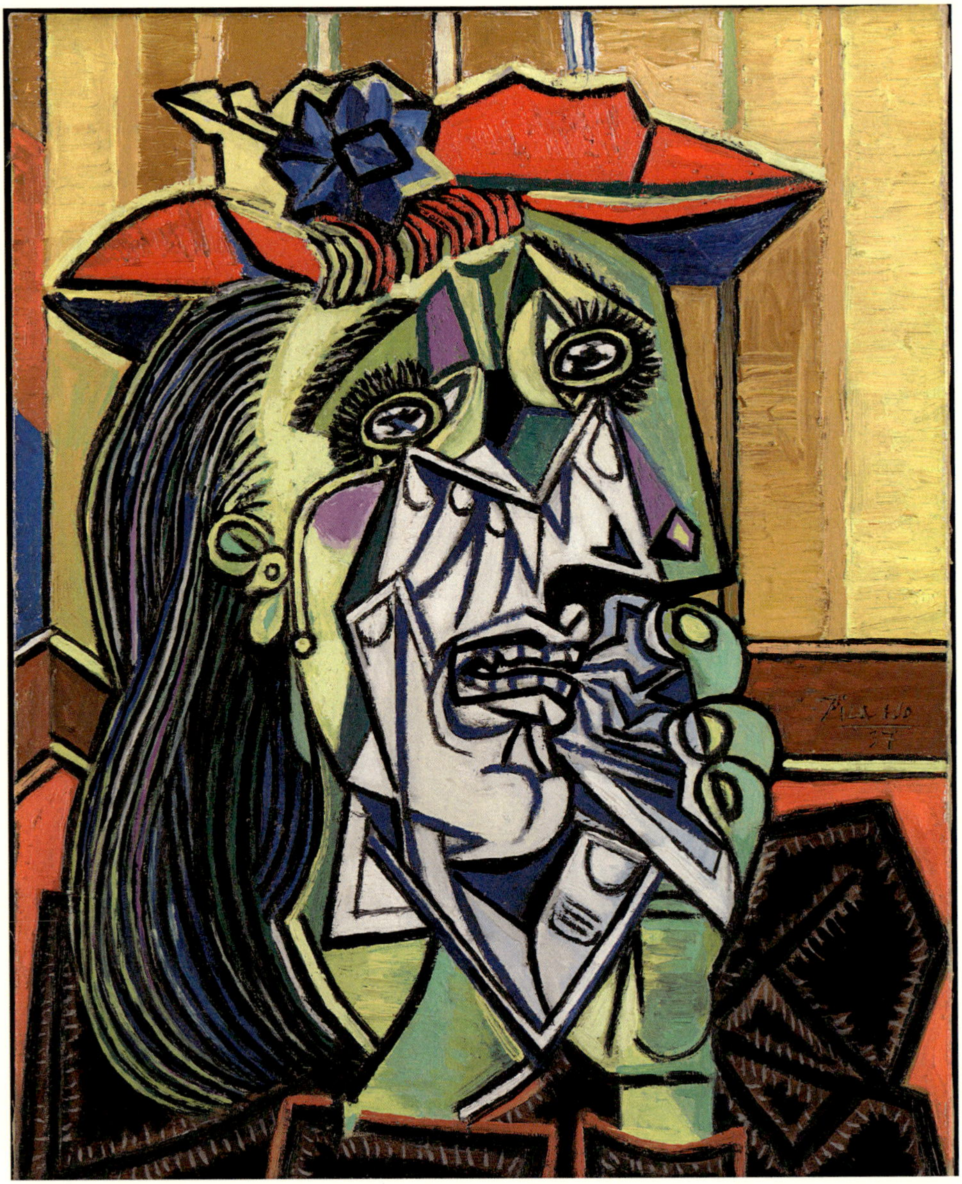

Cubism*

Yesterday her forehead was a clear smoothness, marred
      only by the occasional blemish—benign overflow of life-oil rising to the surface.

Her lashes, all three sets of them, have thinned. Her unibrow's gone gray.
      The eyes beneath thick glasses magnify and retreat, retreat and magnify.

Her face is a rearranged version of what once it was, the whole
      fragmented, the fragments in disarray. Today it is her young nose she misses

most, its reliable line, its precision. Now, it lists to the side, wishing
      it could hide. Even so, it presides. When

did it happen, this disfigurement? She was aging, as they say,
      nicely—lines and white hair advancing millimeter by discreet millimeter.

But today she wakes to mutilated reflection: the parts scattered,
      edges frayed. Here, the sagging contour signifying *jaw*, there

the emaciated stroke of *lip*, pencil thin, reduced to a smear of pink. When
      did it shrink? From the mirror it stares back its answer—eloquent,

alone. Her pouty lower lip abdicated years ago. She forgets what trade she made
      to lose its moody protrusion. Those moods! Where did they go?

She cut them out. Now she wants them back. Bring on the forbidden words. *Tristesse.*
      Melancolia. Retrieve *chagrin.* Get Teutonic. Get guttural.

Remember *Weltschmerz. Torschlusspanik. Lebensmüde.*
 Use tongue, mandible, throat. Use breath. Employ all you know. Find

the missing pieces. Fill in the face. Imagine the whole. Here is the chin. Here
 is the jaw. Here are the lips. Splice back the parts.

Now frown. Now scowl. Grin. Glower. Is this the dream of impossible retrievals?
 Fine: then be the dream.

*after *Weeping Woman* (1937) by Picasso

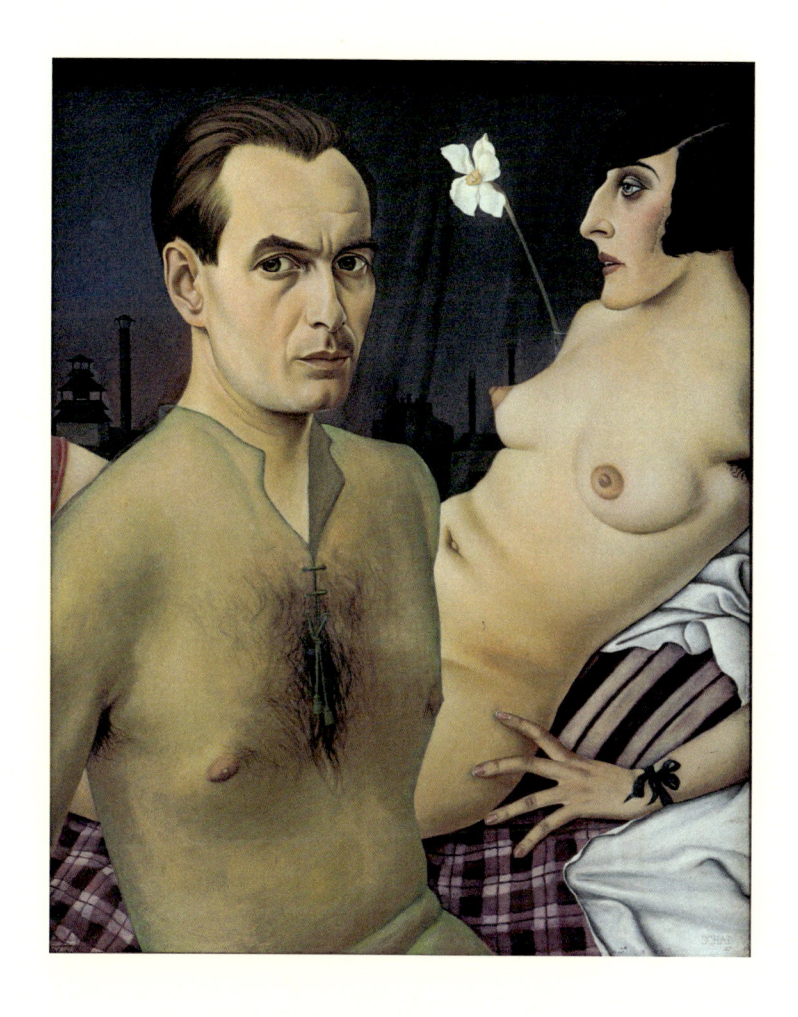

The Model Speaks*

He's a strange one: he likes me nude, but leaves
my red socks on, then ties a ribbon on my wrist.
I could give him more, but he resists.

He studies my profile; focused on my beak, he says
it's *wunderbar, sehr modern*, stylishy severe.
He loves my crimson nails. Maybe he's queer.

Himself he paints in sheer green tulle designed
to make his hair and skin look vegetal. His torso's made of moss.
He wears a cross—

revealing he's a Christian (like his name). He wants
(like me) to be a sinner. But while I sin and sin, he fails.
I strip and call *come here*, but fear—not mine—prevails.

I want him, true, but say *I'm not the whore you take me for*—
words he ignores while twisting my limbs into a pose.
Meanwhile, I take his measure, compose

in verse *his* portrait in my head, though he and I don't rhyme.
Palate in hand, his red brush scars my canvas cheek.
He sees himself as *barbarisch* —a real barbarian—not the meek

artiste I see rapt more with his mirror self than me.
Above us hangs a flower—a narcissus, if I'm correct—
so fragrant I'm aroused. My nipples stand erect.

He's miles away, yet I suggest he take me for the night.
He smiles abstractly in my direction, but past my open thighs,
trapped by his own reflection, his *own* magnetic eyes.

*after *Self-Portrait with Model* (1927) by Christian Schad

Convalescent Woman in a Time of Plague*
—The Harvard Museum, March 10, 2020

By a vase of sagging sunflowers!
That's where you put me?
They droop, they drag their moldy petals
toward me, toward extinction. Confined
to this room, we rot
in our shared condition,
our former radiance impossible to imagine.

Meanwhile, with me against the papered wall, you paint,
enthralled. Decay interests you. Death
interests you more. You watch. You study.
You arrange and re-arrange
and frame and reframe.

And paint—heedless
of your own contagion, infecting
me with your illness. You paint
my living and now
my inexorable dying
into your Art.

In the garden you've placed a Polynesian totem
—my twin! —to keep me company. A kindness
or a joke? To show how uncannily alike
we have become: our wooden skin the same, our chiseled
cheeks and hollow eyes a perfect match, each
the other's mirror—primitive,
forever ornamental, like all your curios:
macabre, silent.

But when the lilacs bloom
into their Springtime raiment she'll be *there*
breathing their magnificence
while I remain *here*
on the other side of the glass, enclosed,
in my pajamas, posing
as myself: a diseased centerpiece for a triptych dedicated to disease.
No wonder passersby recoil at the sight of me—
my sallow skin and fevered cheeks.
The eyes which say it all.

*after *The Convalescent Woman* (1913) by Erich Heckel

Klee in Tunisia*

—April 1914

Thirty-five and burning bright—
a single star, flush
with cultivation, Europe's
age-old tinctures fermenting
inside me:
I am still young.

Around me
other stars shine, spinning
in our shared orbit; we train
our gaze inward, not out,

where the world hurls
toward war.

Our cosmos
is a sandbox
where daily
we play. It is a tiny
mortal universe, not
the vast playground
of the gods. In this space
we toil, sifting
and searching
for something new.

Some days, alone, I am
All angles: stark
and sarcastic.   My laughing
figures go silent. The world
interrupts and the dance turns
macabre. The landscape darkens.
My people shrink
to sticks.

But here my cold sticks warm
in the Tunisian sun. Everything is hot,
curvilinear and fluid. My sticks drink
and drink it in.

Color possesses
them—ochres and jades, faded
magentas and watery blues.

Even the whites
have weight. Here,
the *absence* of color
is still color, deep
in its denials, true.

With my black box
of six colors I record
what I see. It's all I need
to feel complete.
An illusion? Perhaps.
But today at Kairouan
the mosaics and stained glass
yielded to my brush, my paper,
my paint. Only the local beasts
repelled my efforts.

The dwarfed asses
and fly-ridden dromedaries
scare me.
They wander collarless
through the streets,
snorting and dripping
with snot. They honk
and they spit. And they stink.
As do I.

As for the huddled beings
bent in shadow at the souk, swaddled
in robes—only a Giotto
could paint them.

From afar, I admire their bulk,
their enormous simplicity.
But I am bad at bulk
and worse at enormity.

Here at the edge of the Sahara
I am trying to adapt.
But I am little and Swiss
and I resist.

My frugality says no
and no again
to all that is vast,
even the vastly beautiful.

And yet the woman I saw today,
her haik wrapping
and unwrapping, twisting
its folds in the wind,
undid me.

And when the sun pours down
in sheets of gold over these
walls of qallaline and faience, spilling
over turquoise friezes
in a sea of light,
I surrender.

*after *View of Kairouan* (1914) by Paul Klee

Against the Light*

He prefers darkness
to light. Nights
to the tyranny of days

where there is no schedule
to observe. No rules.
No wakeful day-people
to call back, appreciate,
critique. No demands
to answer, love or deplore.

In the great city
though the many are asleep,
the knowing few
come out. He likes
to put on his black trench coat
and cap and walk among
them, incognito. He can stoop
and waver, grab
the banister for balance
without shame. The river is rising
along the embankment
but he fears not the flood.
In the shadows he almost
discerns a tangle of lovers.
By the bridge a young stag
beckons him. He smiles
back but tonight, resists.
The hours of the night
are short but deep
and he is loath
to share their depths.

*after *Quer zum Licht*, by Claus Vogelsang, 1987

Pietà*

This time the migraine came with a vision
bathed in night sweat:

I was sitting on the Eames chair,
your man's body on my lap, legs

and arms white as casein draped over
mine, spilling onto the cassock, new sores

on your legs, dried blood
on your feet and hands,

from your chalk mouth
the words *forgive me,*

from mine, the impossible
no

                                                      *after *Pieta* by Michelangelo, 1497

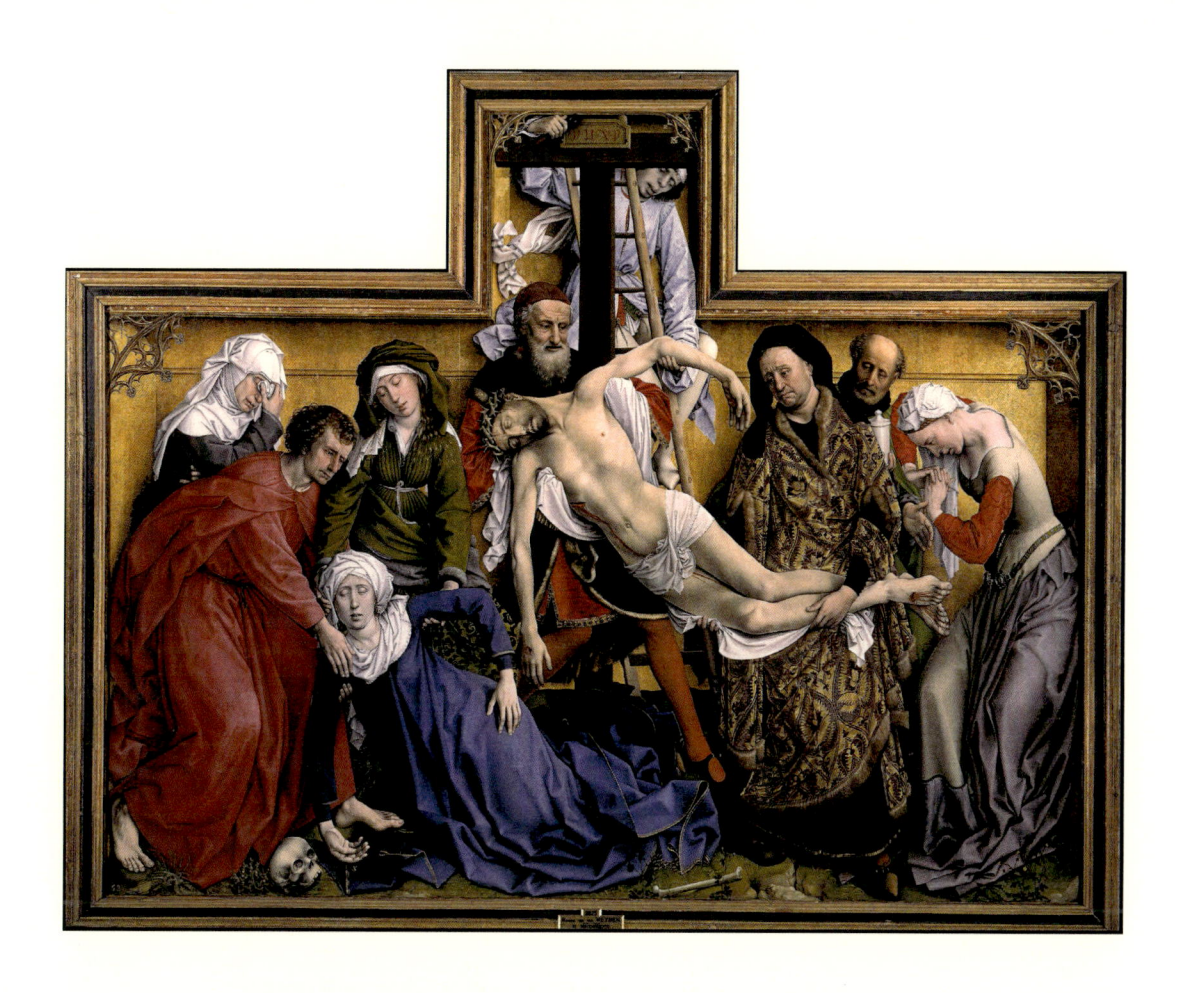

Deposition*

for Matthew Shepard (1976-1996)

I am in the foreground in mid-swoon, still reeling,
blue cloak blowing in the sudden storm.
Darkness obscures the horizon and behind me

a construction site, men on a ladder, the fence
which became your cross—and behind the fence
a church spire

blessing nothing. The sword
which I have always known would pierce my heart
cuts through me.

The young corpse slung
over your father's friend and namesake
is yours.

The pasty boy-flesh stark
against the weathered arms bearing you
is yours.

My women friends are all named Mary. They lean into me,
murmuring Aramaic consolations. Bent in sorrow,
they catch my fall.

A column of light pans the scene from above.
The vast Wyoming sky bursts
with a waterless electric rain.

The Palladian arch framing the scene
contains my grief.
That's how I know this is a dream.

*after *Deposition of Christ* by Rogier van der Weyden, 1435

Frau Dürer on *Melencolia I* *

I know it's you in the gown, aspiring angel,
and this your self pitying self portrait.
Oppressed, stippled, hatched to death,

you are everywhere and not.
No signature, no visible watermark,
no reassuring A over D
to endorse our admiration. Why?
Too blue to sign?
Too intent to blacken every inch with Meaning,
incise every copper line with Sorrow?
Penseroso half-man:
you've succumbed to the bleakest
black humor, the most putrid gall.
Melancolia. Melancolie. Melancholy—
Be *mine*. Not hers,
whoever she is, this mistress you serve
night and day in your studio explaining
the universe. You, who study proportion,
perspective, you have gone too far:
published your confusion for the world to see.

Outgrow the adolescent romance with *misery*,
this dark mask of profundity, compulsive
working up of sadness to impress your intellectual friends.
Line over line over line amassing dejection.
Find a clearing on the page and stay there.
That smooth patch of light on your knee
will do. As a spiritual exercise, leave
the spot untouched, virginal and soft.
Now lighten the rest, neutralize the grays,
push the colonizing blacks back to the border.

Geometry, that god you worship,
has betrayed you. It clutters
your surface with angles and shapes,

tempting you to ponderous speculation, placing
clumsy obstacles in your path.
That rhomboid, for instance: remove it.
Its sole purpose is to create an abyss
for your furtive *putto* should he tumble
from his millstone perch, too absorbed
with his scribbles to notice the threat.

Wipe that scowl off your brow. Pay attention!
The compass on your lap is idle, but one wrong move
and the point will pierce you where it hurts.
Put it down.
Don't you know that happiness is not arrived at
with measure and weight? Or art with contrived ideas?
Throw away your theorems and faddish alchemy.
Resist tedious Allegory.
This print is a treatise.
It has no truth. No grace.

Take St. Luke as your model, ardent
worker in his studio, painting the Virgin,
God guiding his hand.
This can be your fate, too.
Have faith, my husband.
Incessant study has not served you.
Knowledge is a trap, reason the spring.
Go back to craft. Retrieve the lessons of the goldsmith.
Find freedom in convention, relief in labor.
Make art your prayer.

How I long to escape through that hole in the sky!
Just past the bat's tail, beyond twilight.

I pine for that sunny hamlet on the horizon,
lapped by sea, bathed in light. You'll say it's
sheer kitsch, no place for an artist.
But think again.
This city—our Nuremberg—
with its plagues and cerebral temptations
has misled you.
Leave it.

Intimate not mortality, but this present in-itself-ness all around.
Defy that hourglass over your shoulder,
the stupid bell over your head
clanging you to order, the magic calendar on the wall.
Remember: this is a positive print from a negative engraving.
Use now the idle hammer and nails strewn about you, mend
the broken plane on the floor.
Fill in the globe, blank now as heaven.
Make a map, if you must, for us.
Keep Euclid for this practical purpose.

Banish enigma. Forget the labored tomes.
Choose the material world. Choose life.
Lose this exile of thought you made our home.
For once, Albrecht, listen: I am your wife.

*after *Melencolia I* (1513) by Albrecht Dürer

Double Portrait*

In the foreground is her lover's wife,
always and forever in the foreground
stolid and immovable as the afterlife.

She edges into the adjacent space
—almost touching the wife, but not quite—
trying to read her expressionless face.

Set wide in the classical mode and blue, her eyes
stare out and inward under a widow's peak,
arrow pointing at her nose. The wife is wise

to everything—her husband's habits, his feckless
ways, his lover's plump expectancy, wise even
to that barren ball of fur always on her lap, that neckless

tail-less rodent-bitch they call their honey-pooch. She
will not bear pups, though her mistress will. Soon *they*
(the wife tries not to think the pronoun)–no, *she* and *he*

will have a child. The wife is married but alone,
while her own stark womb, buried between hip bones—her
pelvis, her ovaries, her futile uterus—have all turned to stone.

She buries her shame in the pink folds of aristocratic silk;
inherited gold adorns her ears and throat. Nothing to be done
for her forever flat chest: her breasts will never give milk.

The lover almost hears the wife hissing *Beware!*
She will bear his child but never *have* her husband.
She vows to master the expressionless stare.

The wife has neither dog nor heir. But her man is her man.
On her lap is her faithful fan, a tool to cool distemper and desire.
The lover knows and does not know her role in The Plan.

*after *Double Portrait of Frau Swarenski and Carola Netter* (1923) by Max Beckmann

Margherita Sarfatti*
—Roma, 1925

See the happy couple.
Look how we tilt
our heads and vamp
for the camera,
hands on knees, butt thrust
out in mock provocation.

I catch you close your eyes, fake
sleep, adjust your toupee.
Do you never tire of pretense,
the daily travesties, my own darling
Duce, Ducino, Don Benito bello!

Today, we take a day
for clowning — tip-toe
around the tar-black
shadows cast by St. Peter's
over our guilt-defying world.

With bare feet we step
gingerly over its inky
surface as it spreads, staining
and claiming all in its path,
obliterating color, threatening

even our filmy blue horizon.
We repudiate the dark, refuse
the dominant gloom; instead, we fix
our eyes on the obelisk, not the cupola,
worship not the Vatican but bold "Little Boot"

Caligula, who made his horse a Senator
with no apology and ruled Rome with
impunity. Watch now as our own black shadow
imposes its dominion, how it keeps
spreading, spreading.

*after *Roma* (1925) by Hannah Hoch

I Dreamt I Was Tiger*

Not in my Maidenform bra. But braless, wild—with the cold eviscerating stare of a cat on the prowl, alert for the kill. All appetite. No manners.

It is 1965. Sumatra. Island of gold, named by invaders
drunk on panning the banks of the Siak.
I am thirteen—ivory bones and teeth,

jaw and claws of steel, black blood running through me, pumped
by a still fearsome heart. I feel young, but in tiger years
I'm middle-aged and worried about my thinning fur:

my stripes start thick and gleaming but disintegrate
into spots near the end, like a rash. Between
each pair, a cluster of pale freckles.

Where will it end, this fading? Will I go gray and, surviving
into palsied age, turn white? And then? What then? Will
I expire into a colorless vapor? Or burst?

I'd rather eat. It's what we do. Feed till we're sated. No restraints.
Even through sleep a void wants filling. Cliché? Perhaps,
but true. Padding through the forest floor

I binge on monitor lizard, gorge on tree frog, whatever snack crosses
my path. When I trip on a Python pretending to be a log
I succumb to his grip, let him squeeze

me with his cool body, whole and smooth, hard, then harder till
I nearly faint. I like the game, but keep the session short.
My swift bite to his neck finishes it for us both.

A lick of termite off a rotten sandalwood stump cleanses the palate.
Sika, buffalo, and civet never disappoint, but today
my post-python *tristesse* is their friend.

Above, a mossy canopy of pine and oak drips with edible life.
Flying squirrel and chimps tease with celestial chatter.
I resist with ease, preferring earthbound things:

tapir, wild pig, boar. The occasional porcupine—quill-crunch,
meat and bones. Sambar, gibbon and chital are sweet.
But oh my kingdom for a human.

*after *Surprised!* or *Tiger in a Tropical Storm* (1891) by Henri Rousseau

Self-Portrait in a Thriftstore Cap*

Astonished, or pretending to be,
my brows knit
into a question, mouth pursed,
almost open, rounding out an *O
it's you*, a joke, of course
since it is always
you, next to me,
or facing me,
as you are now
with a camera, still

amazingly alive, here, still
tickled to have caught
me trying on this goofy cap
someone's grandma might have knit,
with all the pieces of left-over yarn
in her craft bag, remnants of her devotion.

I ask *is this hideous or wonderful?*
You shake your head at my bad taste, yet
something about this cap
draws me: it is aggressive
and I am not, and wearing it
I am aggressively un-beautiful. Not
an object of desire, but free, just
some nameless dame with her hair up
in a tacky wool cap. No one
to notice or speak to or taunt.
If I am smart I can be smart. Or silly.
Or neither. Soon enough
I will be old, beyond such
remembered oppressions
(youth and its exhausting beauty!)
but now there is the luxury of
pretending to be un-beautiful
—a kind of play within
a play—within a play,
the concluding scene
off-stage, for now deferred.

*after *Self-Portrait in a Cap* (1639) by Rembrandt

Morning Meditation *

Today, my back's to the window.
I have placed my chair against it.

I will not be diverted
by loggias and domes,
or consoled
by the perfection of cupolas.
Do not intrude.
This is my time.
I will close my eyes
and keep perfectly still.
My limbs are limp, ready
for peace.
*Relax
your eyelids*, my memorized
meditation cd commands.
I relax them.
*Relax your jaw,
your neck*—
Step by step, I scan
the tension away.
Smile, says
Thích Nhát Hanh,
his saccharine wisdom
for a moment interrupting
my grim resolve. Obediently,
I smile.
It is only an exercise.
For one minute I can
let myself *be like a pebble
at rest.* Even so,
the winter light keeps
to the exterior. Inside
I mind the dark.

*after *Silvana Cenni* (1922) by Felice Casorati

GARLAND OF CURING RAGAS

42

1.
Safina*

I will, I promise, write it all down
on this long palm leaf with the squid ink you gave me,
but first

let me dip my brush in colors
—vegetal greens and blues—
to make of this troubled year

with its dark inexorable transience
something luminous
and durable.

With vivid pigments I'll take back what was lost, stroking
us in as two stylized rocks, indigo and gray, floating behind
an unfathomably marbleized foreground.

We can't paint precisely
what was this illness, nor
apprehend it with line or perspective.

Instead, let me make something new that is ours.
Not a replica of the past but a safe world
composed of grace.

On parchment I will paint a garden with date palms
and frangipani; border it with acanthus hedge.
Instead of grass, a lawn of chamomile.

On this bed of blue violets we will dream by day
what was almost sorrow into a place of light and wonder.
And by night

(although we are rocks, solid and enduring)
we shall don raiment of magenta and mauve
and dance

atop a colonnade of arches, appeasing
the nocturnal raptor with our song.

*after 16th c. Mughal ragamala painting (Deccan, India)

2.
Falling Peacock in Rainstorm at Night*

My tail of colored feathers
hangs matted
closed behind me

It weighs me down

In this wet darkness
I can neither
dance nor fly

This darkness
weighs me down

No one here
to see my splendor

My only company
the relentless rain

Together
we fall from the sky
toward the darkening wood

The leafy trees below
reach out to catch me
but cannot

Between their outstretched
limbs I travel
like a stone

The swallows
sitting safely in their nests
sleep the sleep of the oblivious

innocent
of cellular divisions
silent metastasis

Their oblivion weighs me down

Only the insomniac owl
watches—alert —
for the kill

My famous feathery tail-eyes
are folded inward
blind to possibility

I am falling   falling away—
When will I escape
this monsoon sickness

Sing me a raga   spin
me a garland
oh earth
but do not yet welcome me

Show me the sun.

* after 16th c. Mughal ragamala painting (Deccan, India)

नटभल्हारिका २

उजलुमधुबनालिकिलुरलटंकेरदेनिमैलेनीरेनीरऊलोचनाचुब्वे तैनानरैपतिदेखानि
कातारेपिकरूडतेसुरवरारेलालता लिखितेच्वानंगमैपतिर्विजयतेमंदेदरदंशनिलैरु
रलूबरधरानत्वानीचकेतुकधारिणी ।। कतकीगनैमोरांगीनटमह्लारिकासट्नाः ।।

3.
Before the Rain at Nat Mahar*

You sit on the shore, enclosed
In your condition—
Aflame, but out of reach.

I am a maiden
Splashing you
From the lotus-filled river.
My silver droplets fly in your direction,
But cannot penetrate
The invisible shield encasing you.

The diagonal axis of the river cuts through me
Yet we are laughing,
The two of us;
We must
Find it all
So terribly funny,
This splashing,
This futile game.

Below, approaching
Bands of worms
Prepare the ground.

Maybe they are not worms at all, I think.
They are the same forms

Giovannni di Paolo painted
In his Creation of the World.
I know them well;
I've known them for years,
Those ominous harbingers
Of our expulsion from Paradise,
Our sudden sentence to rot, to die.

This thought does not console me.
Nor does the next thought, that
I am only dreaming a terrible dream.
Meanwhile, the industrious worms—
So pink and mindless and alive—
Continue their very real labor
Preparing the very real dirt.

      * after 16th c. Mughal ragamala painting (Deccan, India).

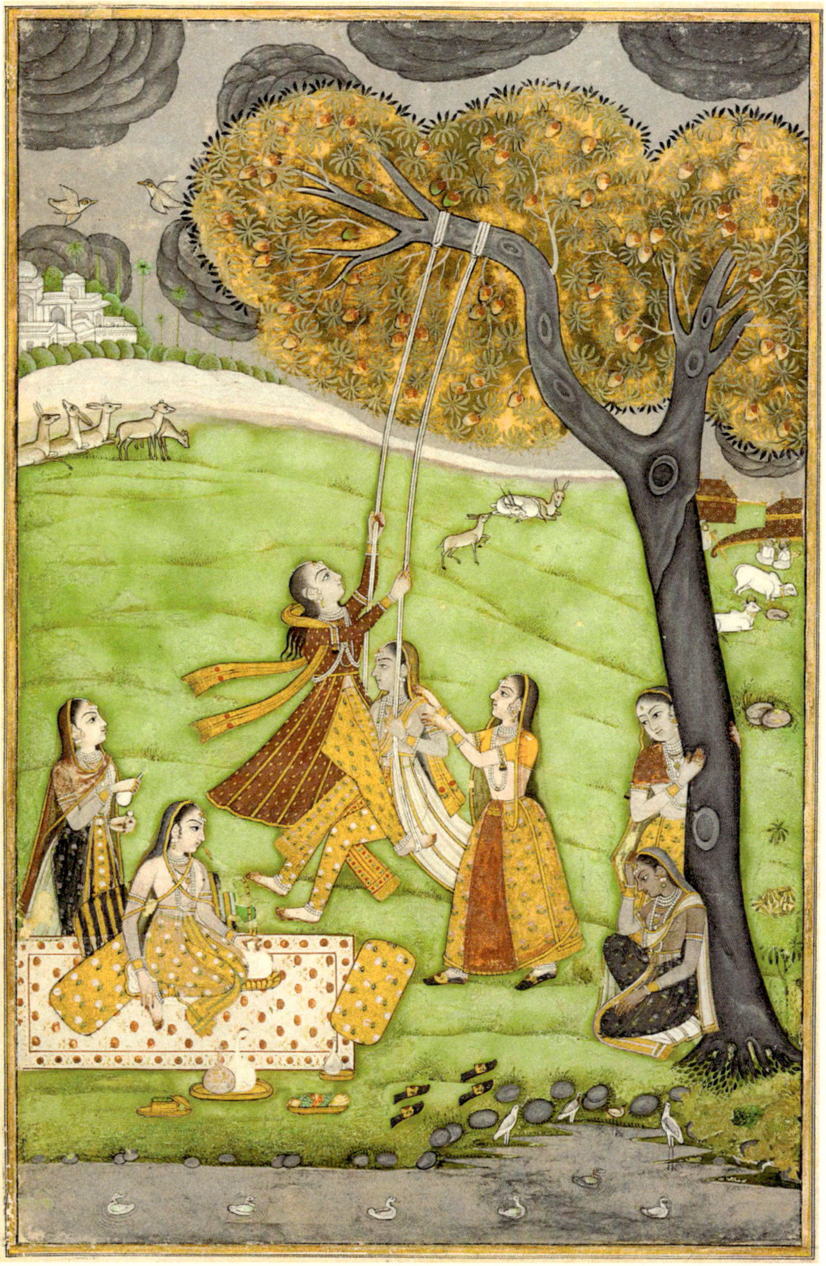

4.
Deccan Picnic with Krishna*

Though he is king he eschews the crown. On occasion
he'll don his feathered dhoti
but today he'd rather play than rule.

Here in the royal meadow the grass is fragrant with clover.
He treads lightly on its purple blossoms.
In the Vedic tradition,

He is the enchanter, but today he too may be enchanted—
his heroism, his divinity, for the time sent on furlough.
He has brought his flute, but left his godly blue skin at home.

Of his 16,000 cow-maidens only a few have gathered here.
He loves us all, but loves me best. I keep to the shadows, let
the others dote on him in the sun, entertain him with their games.

Two pump gaily on a swing suspended from the ancient tree,
their young breasts freely airing in the breeze. Another, laughing,
sings as they swing, *Oh adorable one of the white lily eyes.*

It is mango season again. After a harsh winter, this: ripe fruit cascade
carelessly to the ground. Succulence everywhere.
I have lain out a banquet atop an Agra carpet; our half-naked attendant

further adorns the scene. She pours tea from silver vessels, extends
a cup to her lord. Her hennaed toes pull his gaze
the length of her body; he receives the drink, gives her a flower

in return. How sweet, how gallant is my king, I think,
then avert my stare, return to my place in the shade. It is cool
here under the mango tree and I am too sleepy for dark thoughts.

My king is back and he is happy. This is my mantra.
Behind me the old cows lie in the sun, their empty udders
tucked neatly beneath them.

Not so sad to be old and dry, I think,
as long as we are considered sacred.

* Ladies on a Swing (c.1750), Anonymous, Mughal ragamala painting (Deccan, India)

The Last Wait *

Between wall and wall
tucked tight in your bed
you wait, wishing
not to wake
     —let this be the night—

but with dawn your eyes open
and you find yourself
here. Awake.

You cannot finish what's begun.

You rot
from outside in: first
the skin, once
a burnished olive—
radiant and smooth—
now blistered, blighted
with moles.
Next the bones
gone soft, flesh loosed
over dissolving armature.
Your fingers by now
useless digits, right shoulder
an agony, arrested
in a remorseless hunch.
When I turn you,
you want to cry out
but hold back, hold out.

Inside the porous, wasted shell
the dignified will
insists, lifts its cureless
head, refuses
one last time
to give in.

At ninety, you
say *no* to everything
unbeautiful and unkempt,
keep your vigil, comb your hair,
moisten your own sweet lips
and wait,
for death, for dinner:
whichever comes first.

The meal arrives, sautéed liver
and onions: *fegato a la veneziana*,
you say, the Italian still
there, cheering you for a moment,
distracting you from your desire
to die (or is it my desire,
my impatience, more than yours?)
and I say *don't*,
don't eat it, Mamita, let it go,
satisfy your body's
other hunger,
to be done, out
of all this now. Over.
You smile weakly,
in agreement,
and eat.

*after *Portrait of the Artist's Mother* (1989) by Lucien Freud

The Fate of Pleasure*

Hardly native and far from naked, these dignified
loungers by the Hudson stroll in their Sunday best,
white as the lilies in the foreground, white
as the sails on the little boats below
navigating the river, white as the scentless smoke
pluming up from the passing steamboat. In this Sunday idyll

the mill's emissions across the way seem to our idle
onlookers harmless, improbably elegant, dignified.
Such feathery streams of benign smoke
are sure signs of a singular prosperity. All the best
families know this. No need to consider what below
the smoke burns, what beneath the river's crisp white

crests gathers and congeals. Above, the white
surface and the complacent sense of an afternoon idyll
in the park where leisure reigns are all that matter. Below
the presiding sycamore a boy crouches, rather undignified
but engaged in addressing a cat trying her best
to look like a dog. Why notice the forbidden smoke

from his Southern cousin facing the tree? Discreet with his smoke
he turns away so it dissolves invisibly in the white
clouds above. His father is fresh from Havana with cigars and sugar, the best
available. New cargo will replace the old: Runaways enjoying their newfound idyll
make easy marks. He lures them with lies, promises of protection, a dignified
life. He'll keep a few, chain the rest. The catch of the day he'll stash below—

necessarily confined to reside below
in the dank, unlit hull, darkness like their skin, darker than smoke,
dark as their master's satin top hat, upright and dignified
on his proud Southern head, dark even as his patent boots. His white
masterly jaw under a full, black mustache stays clenched against all idle-
ness, though today he's agreed to give his Yankee wife the best

hours of the day, strolling without purpose among the best
families of the faultless town. His mind strays to the cargo below,
the price it will fetch in Charleston; he smiles at the way his idle
son hides his new habit, blowing into the sycamore the smoke
from the puro he stole from the Havana cache, his white
shirt immaculate, his wiles instinctual, integral as his gloves to his dignified

Sunday best. Though it is the Sabbath and the mill across the river below is idle,
its spindles still, our languorous strollers ignore the anomalous smoke
spreading—relentless, white—across the sky on this dignified day of rest.

*after *Outing on the Hudson* (c. 1850), Anonymous

NOTES

p. 25
Matthew Shepard was born in Caspar, Wyoming in 1976. He was a gay college student at the University of Wyoming who was beaten, tortured, tied to a fence and left to die there in Laramie, Wyoming, 1996.

p. 31
When Max Beckmann was commissioned in 1923 by Georg Swarenski, the director of the Städel Museum in Frankfurt, to paint a portrait of his wife, Beckmann asked Swarenski's mistress, Carola Netter, to pose for him separately so that he could then put the two women together in this painting. When Beckmann gave the double portrait to the collection, the museum was forced to accept the gift so as to keep the painting out of circulation, away from the eyes of Swarenski's wife.

p. 33
Margherita Sarfatti was one of Mussolini's several mistresses.

p. 42-53
These poems were written at a time when the author's husband was briefly but seriously ill and receiving treatment in New York City. During those months there was an important exhibition at the Metropolitan Museum of Art of paintings from Deccan, India, including several illustrations from song books of curing ragas.

p. 57
This poem was commissioned by Thomas S. W. Lewis for an exhibition on the Hudson River at the Tang Museum at Skidmore College.

CREDITS

Giorgione. *La Tempesta.* c. 1508 / Public Domain, via Wikimedia Commons

Edouard Vuillard. *The Album.* 1895. The Metropolitan Museum of Art, New York. © 2021 Artists Rights Society (ARS), New York. Photo: © The Metropolitan Museum of Art / Art Resource, New York

Felice Casorati. *Le Signorine.* 1912. Galleria Nazionale d'Arte Moderna, Venice. © 2021 Artists Rights Society (ARS), New York / SIAE, Rome. Photo: Cameraphoto Arte, Venice / Art Resource, New York

Pablo Picasso. *Weeping Woman.* 1937. Tate, London. © 2021 Estate of Pablo Picasso / Artists Rights Society (ARS), New York. Photo: © Tate Photography

Christian Schad. *Self-Portrait.* 1927. Tate, London. © 2021 Christian Schad Stiftung Aschaffenburg / ARS, New York / VG Bild-Kunst, Bonn. Photo: © Tate Photography

Erich Heckel. *To the Convalescent Woman.* 1912-13. Harvard Art Museums/Busch-Reisinger Museum, Edmée Busch Greenough Fund © 2021 Artists Rights Society (ARS), New York / VG Bild-Kunst, Bonn. Photo: ©President and Fellows of Harvard College

Paul Klee. *View of Kirwan.* 1914. Permanent Private Loan, Collection Rudolf Ibach, Franz Marc Museum, Kochel am See. © 2021 Artists Rights Society (ARS), New York. Photo: collecto.art and Franz Marc Museum

Klaus Vogelgesang. *Quer zum Licht.* 1987. Berlinische Galerie, Berlin. Courtesy Klaus Vogelgesang. Photo: Kai-Annett Becker/Berlinische Galerie

Michelangelo. *Pietà.* 1498-99 / CC BY-SA 3.0, via Wikimedia Commons

Rogier van der Weyden. *Descent from the Cross*. Before 1443. Museo del Prado, Madrid / Public Domain, via Wikimedia Commons

Albrecht Dürer. *Melencholia I*. 1513 / Public Domain, via The Metropolitan Museum of Art

Max Beckmann. *Double-Portrait*. 1925. Städel Museum, Frankfurt. © 2021 Artists Rights Society (ARS), New York. Photo: bpk Bildagentur / Städel Museum / Ursula Edelmann / Art Resource, NY

Hannah Höch. *Roma*. 1925. Berlinische Galerie, Berlin. © 2021 Artists Rights Society (ARS), New York / VG Bild-Kunst, Bonn. Photo: Kai-Annett Becker/ Berlinische Galerie

Henri Rousseau. *Surprised!* 1891. National Gallery, London. Photo: © National Gallery, London and Art Resource, NY

Rembrandt van Rijn. *Self-Portrait in a Cap*. 1630. Courtesy National Gallery of Art, Washington

Felice Casorati. *Silvana Cenni*. n.d. Private Collection, Turin. © 2021 Artists Rights Society (ARS), New York / SIAE, Rome. Photo: Bridgeman-Giraudon / Art Resource, New York

Gauri Ragini, First Wife of Malkos Raga, Folio from a *Ragamala (Garland of Melodies)*. 1575-1600. Los Angeles County Museum of Art, Bequest of Edwin Binney, 3rd (M.90.141.2). Photo: © Museum Associates/ LACMA.

Peacock in a Rainstorm at Night. Late 16th c. Private Collection, London

Nat Malhar: A Woman Splashing Water on her Lover from the River. Late 16th c. Private Collection, London

Ladies on a Swing. Mid-18th c. Private Collection / Bridgeman Images

Lucian Freud. *The Painter's Mother Resting I.* 1976. Private Collection © The Lucian Freud Archive / Bridgeman Images

Outing on the Hudson. c. 1875, The Colonial Williamsburg Foundation, Williamsburg. VA. From the collection of Abby Aldrich Rockefeller; gift of the Museum of Modern Art.

ACKNOWLEDGEMENTS

"Frau Dürer on *Melencolia I*" appeared in *Raritan.*

"The Fate of Pleasure" appeared in *Slate* and in *Lives on the Hudson,* the catalogue for an exhibition at the Tang Museum.

"La Tempesta" appeared in *To Forget Venice.*

"Cubism" and "Against the Light" appeared in *La Presa.*

"Pietà" appeared in *Ontario Review* and in *Honey with Tobacco.*

"Deposition" appeared in *Paris Review* and in *Honey with Tobacco.*

"Falling Peacock in the Rain" appeared in *Poetry Daily.*

"Safina," "Before the Rain at Nat Mahar" and "Deccan Picnic with Krishna" appeared in *La Presa.*

ABOUT THE AUTHOR

PEG BOYERS is Executive Editor of *Salmagundi* magazine and the author of three previous books of poetry published by the University of Chicago Press: HARD BREAD (2002), HONEY WITH TOBACCO (2007) and TO FORGET VENICE (2014). She teaches poetry at Skidmore College and at The New York State Summer Writers Institute, and has taught workshops in translation at The Columbia University School of the Arts. Her poems regularly appear in such magazines as *The New Republic, Paris Review, Harvard Review* and many others. Her recent work includes a series of poems in the journal *Liberties* and the afterword to the New York Review of Books edition of Natalia Ginzburg's *Family Lexicon*.

For the full Dos Madres Press catalog:
www.dosmadres.com